Madre Dura

Melody Wilson

LILY POETRY REVIEW BOOKS

Copyright © 2026 by Melody Wilson

All rights reserved. Published in the United States by Lily Poetry Review Books.

Library of Congress Control Number: 2026931727

Cover design and layout: Michael McInnis.
Image from the collection of Lauren Leja, used with permission.

ISBN: 978-1-957755-71-7

Published by Lily Poetry Review Books
223 Winter Street
Whitman, MA 02382
lilypoetryreview.blog/

*For Susan, first of six sisters who fearlessly led us
from where we began to what we became.*

***

With gratitude

To all my teachers, but particularly Kwame Dawes, Joseph Millar,
Ellen Bass, and Danusha Lameris.

Gratitude also to my many poetry sisters: Paulann Petersen, my first
champion this round, and, of course Eileen Cleary for seeing something
here. To the women of Zalon for wading in with sensitivity, wit, and
occasionally, tweezers.

And to Annette Sisson, my poetry partner these years.
What a gift.

***

For my daughters and my husband.
Each of you is everything to me.

Contents

Madre Dura

Self-Portrait with Spanish Mustang

Standing on a berm in the big corral,
I grasp the round bones
of the little mare's jaw,
draw the caramel plane of her nose
to my lips. Her name is Ibeza
and we're a long way from Arizona
where her ancestors slipped away
from *vaqueros* decades and decades ago.
Other mustangs shift and snort
as the seller bemoans the roundup,
the struggles since last year's flood,
the rising price of hay.

Her long head relaxes into my hands,
breath damps the skin of my chest.
She stamps her foot to dislodge a fly,
blows satisfaction. I've come here
knowing I can't take her home
but don't say so. The blood that pumps
through us both once travelled in Iberian ships
though only one of us got away.
I trace the long veins that wind beneath her skin.

I

La Línea

Linda Louise brushes her auburn hair,
dead ringer for our *abuela,* Clara Louise.

Clara's *abuela* was *Maria Luisa.*
Tongues thicken as bloodlines thin.

I am thinking in grandmothers,
unwinding *la línea* to where

hombres traded daughters to *amigos*
like sheep, gave them *nombre blanco*

after *nombre blanco* because
blood is cheaper than land. I'm thinking

en abuelas who clung to *la línea* in code.
Maria becomes Mary, *Luisa* Louise.

Mi Madre era una loca, insisted
I roll my R's, wielded papers to prove

la línea: "My great, great *abuelo, Agustín Olvera,"*
she told grocery, gas station clerks,

"was first judge *de la Ciudad de Los Angeles."*
Mi madre sold the papers to Cal Berkeley.

They're filed under my father's *nombre blanco.*
When *mi madre* told the story of her mother

"closing the track at *Agua Caliente,*"
what she meant to reclaim was the land.

But I picture *mi abuela,* a woman
muy pequeña, banging her handbag

on a gate. The racetrack runs
along the shore, the sand,

caliente as blood, dissolves
beneath my white feet.

All mothers are mythologies

feathery fables with tongues.
Some glide on glassy ponds,

a cygnet beneath each wing.
Others deposit one blue egg

on its father's feet and migrate
away. Mine was a condor,

subsisted on carrion. I didn't know
she teetered between brilliant

and extinct until she hoisted me
to my grandmother's casket,

insisted, *kiss her goodbye.*
I couldn't yet measure

the distances of death,
but tasted the grief gurgling

in my mother's unbeautiful throat.
Even the shade of a wingspan like that

is fleeting. Best to swallow whole
whatever comes from her mouth.

Two Glass Fish

Mama honks until the screen door slams
and Nana scurries down, quilted robe flapping,

leads me into the still-dark room, slips
my sneakers off, then cranks the curtains

before fluttering toward the other room.
On the coffee table, two glass fish balance

on the slender tips of their fins,
clear as water except a blue swirl in the belly

of one, green in the other. I squat between
table and couch, reach a finger out to feel

how cold they are. Through them Nana gusts
refrigerator to stove as if trailing ribbons

of green and blue, sings *Mi hija, come in.*
Light sighs through white curtains

beside the red dinette. Batter sizzles as it hits
the griddle. The bones of her wrist twist the spatula,

flip and flip as she tells a story – about the weather
or her brother. Syrup sticky in its house-shaped tin,

pink curlers in her hair, *siéntate, mantequilla,* a voice
so delicate all I remember is bubbles rising, frozen in glass.

Viceroy

It is a particular privilege,
being asked to pull
the slender ribbon of gold,
lift the cellophane
from my mother's Viceroys.
I unfold the foil corner,
unveiling a row of cylinders
robed in tan paper,
press my nose to the pack –
floral with metal on the tongue.

She smacks the pack
against her fist, propels
a cigarette out, lights it,
one quick drag – one long one,
exhaling, she settles it into her
green ashtray, resumes typing.

A column of ash climbs
from the tip's amber crackle
as smoke rises between us.
I watch her work from beyond
the veil, take so much from her –
how her hands move,
her compulsion to burn.

Chosen Few

Girls who believed in god had cupcakes
in their lunches. Their weeks ascended
in a liturgy of catechism, choir,
Sunday School, mass. I wished
I was the kind of girl who had a special dress
for church. They were probably
already praying when our old Cadillac
lurched to a stop at the Arco Station.

My mother muscled the window down
and lilted to the man, *$10 regular please.*
He jammed the nozzle into the tank
and handed her a cellophane bag.
She passed it to me and I tore it
with my teeth, removed two sheep, one male,
one female, traced the crevices
of their cloven hooves with my nail

while she started talking. By the time
I had posed them on the seat, she'd unfurled
a cascade of photos in plastic sleeves –
daughters, granddaughters, and the clerk
was side-eyeing the highway for customers,
aching for the ding, ding, ding of a rush.

She never said the police brought my sister home
again last night or my father knocked over
the neighbor's fence with his truck.
For as long as she talked, I studied the ark
displayed on the windowsill beside jugs
of antifreeze. Camels, giraffes, a pair of kangaroos
assembled before its ramp. How did he choose?

I imagine small wet heads bobbing in dark water
as the boat rose. There were so many – we had four dogs,
the cat had kittens just last week. I had five sisters.
Before I could ask, my mother started the car.
Next stop was the butcher. If I was good,
I could have a pickle.

How Long it Takes to Change Everything

He presses the Seconal into Mama's hand.
        She puts them in her mouth, swallows,
                deflates into their bed, waits

for them to work. There's no air in the house
        as if the clocks have stopped and the dogs
                have all died. The birds have quit;

the wind has paused. The house is teal,
        the pills are red, the car is dull
                and brown. I stand beside it,

study the hood. Two dents, one deep,
        one shallow. The cracked windshield.
                Our father, frantic, asks my sister:

How fast? She doesn't know. *How many seconds?*
        She doesn't know. He claps time: *one thousand one,*
                one thousand two. He says *newspapers*

and *lawyers, accident* and *court.* He says *manslaughter.*
        The night before, in the back seat,
                still in my Girl Scout uniform,

I do not see, but feel the jolt, hear the thud
        a woman makes striking the hood
                of a car, hurtling over the windshield,

blotting out streetlights. I turn in my seat
      as she scrapes across the roof, slides down
           the rear window into the street.

II

Metaphor

The backgrounds were brown or gray,
the bobbins that hung from the work
blue, yellow, green. Argyle, intarsia,
black skunks with rhinestone eyes,
every knit, every purl an instant
of desire. In the evenings, her hands
were busy making our father's socks
while we unspooled from deep in her past.

We still take turns describing what happened,
pluck at each other's stories, add a knot, a twist,
until truth is so tangled it doesn't matter anymore.
The truth is, our father was a saint. But all my life,
when anyone asked, I said, *my mother was a monster.*
I've heard metaphor is a lie. I don't know anymore.
She loved him. We were the price she paid.

Beautiful from a Distance

My first bra was small and red.
My sister tucked it into her pants at Kmart.
It had no hooks but slipped over my head
in a trapeze act of slender straps,
its sole purpose to give boys something to snap.
Our mother never knew. We had fallen that far
from the gray brassieres coiled in her drawer
like tarps riddled with grommets and struts,
each as solid as the underneath
of a suspension bridge.
I'm afraid of bridges, don't trust rivets
to hold everything up, the way kissing
my mother goodnight didn't make me love her
as much as I wanted to. She was beautiful
in photos and from a distance,
architecture of motherhood.
Even without mastering mathematics,
the force that holds weight in the air.

Undertow

Newspaper crumpling. My sister
sops vinegar up from a bowl,
the window squeaks as she scrubs,
blurring the world outside.

She's taller than me, even on her knees,
hair back, jaw set as her hand
circles then dips, circles then dips,
stops. Even I can see she's distracted

from the messy house by sunlight
sliding through glass in long angular plates
as if life is about to bloom.
The ice in our mother's glass shifts

and my sister's braid sways.
Her slender arm returns
to circling. I have no idea
who I will be without her.

Every Morning Leda

The first home I owned after a series of disasters
had stood empty for a year. Bobcats peered in
as I unpacked, and the howling turned out to be
coyotes, not a woman down the road.
I stood there, gazing out the window
of my own kitchen when a bird so white,
so enormous, stroked by, I could have
counted its feathers if I'd believed it was true.
Then gone.

Impossible. Like the swan
on the cover of my big sister's daughter's
Mother Goose. Bespectacled granny, smiling.
The baby reaching. Such an assumption. I was jealous,
I admit it – stole into the room when they visited.
At twelve, I had nothing left to do but
switch off the lights each night
once our parents extinguished themselves,
so I swallowed one of her Flintstones vitamins –
brightly colored artifact of care.
Then another. Now I know

the bird on the book is just a goose. The old woman
probably a carnie. Swans make awful noises
and each of their toes ends in a claw.
It was a long time before I learned
young girls are covered in scratches.
No one tells you.

Verge

— Jackson, Mississippi 1975

The flour had weevils
though I noticed too late.
I spent most of my days
watching summer shrink
beyond bent Venetian blinds.
At night I perched on the curb
out front of my sister's duplex
strobing my long blonde hair
shoulder to shoulder like a lure,
legs cast into the street
toward Battlefield Park.
I never considered
what would happen
if I ever got it right,
if a truck didn't just slow,
but stopped.
Playground swings dangled
across the way,
their chains shivering light,
but something had tipped
and I didn't care anymore.
Soon I'd be back in California
in the amber glare
of my mother's eyes.
I must have said *yes*
when my sister asked

if I could bake,
showed me the cookbook
and left for work.
I noticed motion in the flour
cleaning up, frosted the cake
anyway. I was afraid
someone might notice, but no one did.
No one noticed anything at all.

Shatter and Boom

The year my father woke to pluck spiders from the air
and my mother slept and slept, I dangled
at the end of a chain of loose relations
where one more teenager wouldn't matter,
where the air was thick and the sky twitched
and warmed to a storm. I spent afternoons
on a porch swing, lost in the clean pages of a romance
about a girl in love with a soldier, didn't hear the car
until the door banged shut and a blonde boy got out
smiling. He was the one who'd been *away at camp*.
I sat up, pulled my hair over my shoulder, made space
for him on the seat. He laughed at my sweating,
said the buzzing was cicadas, said I'd get used to it,
said I could lay my head in his lap. I closed my eyes,
he pulled his fingers through my hair, said,
I could fall for you. When it started to thunder
we ran inside and he said it again,
unbuckling his jeans, letting them fall
to the floor. All I wanted was for him to
say it again, can't remember how long
I watched the chair he'd wedged against the door.
Every few seconds the window lit up.
It flashed and I counted, one thousand two,
one thousand three, one thousand four.

Blue Jeans Blues

Another thing I learned that summer
was that some counties are dry and some are wet,
and you get from one to another by crossing pontoon bridges
that float on the surface of the Homochitto River.
He was backup quarterback and I was a girl
from California. He knew every dirt road
that wound across the Mississippi dark. ZZ Top
thumping, slippery fish of a bridge shimmering
in the dim, I had just enough time to rehearse
drowning before his gold Le Mans
lurched onto shore, a ribbon of cigarette smoke
trailing one side of the river to the other.
Then we were parked by a wooden porch
where half a dozen backlit men bought bootleg beer
and dangled their after-work legs from its edge.
I watched from the passenger seat as he cracked a can,
the tip of his cigarette, red then gone. He pointed to the car,
ducked his head as the other men laughed,
tucked a six pack under his arm. That was the night
I told him I would die by seventeen, mouthed along
to songs I really didn't know, because I liked how his arm felt
draped over my shoulder, how the headlights bored holes in the dark.

Vigil at Seventeen

I watch through glass as the machines
quit breathing. I'd driven down from Salinas
the night before to lay my hand, one last time
on your chest. My sisters take their places
beside your bed as I slip out the door
to watch alone.

No one tries to stop me. I expected
equipment to rattle, the floor to tilt
but the doctor toggles a green lever,
the beeping stops, the ventilator
wheezes to silent.

Now I'm hand over hand on a rope
fraying down a well. All I have
is the *whish* of tires on Hwy 14,
windows rolled down for the breeze,
Daddy at the wheel as you spin
in your seat, pinch my chin in your left hand,
lick your right thumb, scrub at my cheek.
There, you say. *You'll be alright.*

Madre Dura

I think of you in stars, and sometimes shit;
the stars illuminate the clutter of your mind,
the shit is in the pickle aisle. It was years
since your edges softened. I was youngest,
liked you suddenly at my mercy,
so when my father refused, I defied him,
wheeled you to the store, pushed your chair
butcher to baker teasing as I chose the turns.
For a moment we laughed –
but the gasp as you reached for olives,
felt your body fail, the odor, the shame
as you glanced to me for help –
the bolts of heaven rattling loose.
I've been making excuses for you
since I could speak.
Conceded to the chorus of victims,
even imagined wishing you away –
as if I preferred a tepid sky,
as if a meteor shower
isn't worth the burn.
As if I blamed you,
but I lied, I lied.

III

PFC's Tea House

I was twelve the last time we went. The old Cadillac
sailed down the blacktop fissure in the sand
from the stop sign at Avenue N. By then
houses had been built on the right, the desert

to our left remained open, dotted with spring
tumbleweeds – tender and green all the way
to the tips. We could see PFC's for miles,
the neon sign shimmering like the

half-hearted pinnacle of your empty afternoon.
You steered, bare arm out the window, smoked
Viceroys all the way, ordered paper wrapped
chicken, butterflied shrimp, sweet and sour.

I ate rice and almond cookies, sipped tea
from a palm-sized cup, left a slurry of sugar
in the bottom. I still see gold tassels
dangling from paper lanterns above each booth –

taste too-sweet oolong. Today I'm sixty
and you're still forty-nine. So much to say –
I don't bother and focus on what followed,
describe my life at forty, fifty, fifty-five,

talk about my daughters *who can barely*
make tamales, then lean in close to feel
the fibers of your voice as you tell me again
about Tijuana, your mother's tiny feet, the sequins

on your half-sister's dress. Before the check arrives,
I ask the question: *Why can't I name the smell*
that stops me sometimes? Not quite shellfish,
not perfume.

Origin Story

My daughters are women now with children
and jobs, but this spring evening they sit together
on a sofa beneath the red maple, pluck helicopter seeds

from each other's hair. I claim the chair facing them
and settle in before the moment passes. I have done
everything I can do.

This morning I rifled old photos, and none shows
the two of us together, as if our bodies parted
without touching, as if I'd tumbled from the sky

like a legend or a jacaranda seed. I wanted evidence,
a black and white of you braiding my hair,
holding a spoon to my lips.

When the sun begins to set my oldest ignites the flame
that spans the center of the table between us.
It flickers in corners of laughing eyes, makes the ring

on my youngest sparkle. The oldest turns to listen
while the middle daughter smiles into the fire – elbows
fanned out past her ears, fingers laced behind her neck.

Did I say they are beautiful? I wonder where they came from,
how much of them is me, how much of me is you. The youngest
and oldest sip from slender cans of White Claw. What did you see

when you looked at me, still so wild at the end? Did you feel
trunk-heavy, rooted deep in the dark everyone around you
pressed toward sky?

They laugh beyond the margin of fire. One slaps a mosquito,
her sister squeals. The sun drops behind the trees –
there's just enough light to watch them flutter.

Six Inches of Light

We're leaving the party early
so my daughter hands me a packet

of truffles too dark for anyone else.
I open my arms for a hug, awkward

as ever. When the nurse settled her
into my arms I was sixteen,

the room dark except for a sliver left behind
when the door hadn't closed.

I wanted to study her fingers and toes
though I knew I could never swaddle her

so perfectly again. She had passed through
my body and now I was propped up

but slipping. Not yet a mother,
no longer a girl, I wanted

to put her back, the two of us
in one shell. When the nurse returned,

she scooched her up, untied my gown.
Let her cheek brush the nipple,

she said. I cupped her head
and pressed her to my breast.

Her eyes opened, slow and blue,
then closed. The next day, or the next,

I learned to feed her, change her,
tuck the corner of her blanket

under her shoulder.
When I reach for her now

I'm still grasping at light.

At the Aquarium

Tired of dangling her fingers
among anemones, petting sea stars'
sandy backs, my daughter points
to the octopus.

The hall is quiet, so I dangle her
over the open pool, tip her fingers in.
The octopus, magenta but blanching,
sluices to the far side of her acrylic tank,

then back, unfolds three pink tentacles,
each thick as my wrist. One brushes
my daughter's thigh, its tip curling
to beckon, *come closer.*

I've never liked hugging strangers.
A therapist could explain, but why?
I pull my daughter out of reach
and all three tentacles pause

rebuffed, roll into the water like tide
going out. I wish I'd allowed the embrace,
let my daughter know what it's like
wrapped in all those arms, the shell of her ear

pressed against the heart, not the one
thumping landlocked in my chest,
three wet hearts willing to risk
a world for her.

Fledgling

Neither of us can stand the muffled struggle
between the studs. The bird flaps frantic,
ten seconds, fifteen, stops. Ear to wallpaper,
you insist you still hear chirps.

Even to myself I sound like I'm lying –
animals don't know about death.
It continues to fight. We sit on the carpet,
backs to the wall. The bird pauses.
With each interval we hold our breath.

You are almost beautiful, freckled
from summers standing in streams,
studying beetles, weighing the world,
its soft and rough edges. So it hurts to hear
your long exhale, *it's going to die.*
How long will it take? Two nights? Three?
Afternoon glistens on your downy legs.

I swing the pry bar while you break sheet rock
with your hands, thrust shoulder-deep into the hole,
twist to reach. The bird thrashes as you pin its wings,
whisper into your palms.

What you promise, rushing toward the yard
is not for me. I sit alone on the chalky rug, listen
as you open the door, wonder if I'll ever be good enough
to let you go.

Event Horizon

We're in the car, just parked
when my daughter laughs and says,

don't just smear it on. My tube
of Angel Red freezes. I study her

in the narrow field of the rear view,
exhale. It's like that sometimes,

the edge of something rushing
toward you, when the flimsy line

between past and future floats up
from the backseat, a teenager

dabbing lip gloss, dab, dab,
across her smile, *like this*, she says,

then pops her lips. Like reaching
into the shoebox of her past, dried stub

of umbilical cord, stained stuffies,
a poorly shorn Barbie, forfeited

belly-button ring. Today, at 38,
she wears a black sheath and pumps,

tells me not to worry, my event horizon
still so far in the distance. Next week

she'll travel on business while I watch
through a crack in my life – the world

so much bigger on the other side.

Nothing Else Matters

Think of a boat made of milk cartons and duct tape.
My daughter, eleven years old atop this waxy skiff,
plastic paddle – right left, right left, her face
faking bravado. My error is obvious
when other girls blow by with aluminum hulls
and sculling oars. Is this the biggest mistake
I made as a mother? Maybe the Halloween
I dressed her in black, fitted a jute wig
and sent her as *Angst*. Maybe my hurry –
ice cream in a tiny pink spoon, each slip
through her lips savored as I watched
it slide down her long pale throat.

She turned forty last month and yesterday
on the phone, I said *you're probably happy
as you'll ever be*. I'm trying. I am.
But there's a wooly thing grumbling inside
about risk with only this paw to bat her forward.
Animal fear, the way the moon wanes
for wolves, the way a daughter slips like light.

She texts me a cello cover of a Metallica song.
Listen, she says, so I do. Notes tiptoe
on plucked strings, one throaty voice rises,
then another. A song I should know
but don't quite – soft and green as deep woods.
I try and try but will never remember the name.

Souvenir for Mabel

Ortega Trading Post, San Juan Capistrano, 1966 and 2024

Just before you give up, a doll catches your eye,
cornhusk flamenco dancer – slender arms aloft,
face blank as sand, miniature mantilla
the burnt umber of your granddaughter's hair.
Your hand stutters reaching toward the shelf,
breath hitches. Maybe it's the map of cracks
lining the concrete floor just as they did
when your mother warned the three of you
to behave. She nods to the clerk
and leaves you there where your sisters
drag you shelf to shelf fondling turquoise beads
as your neck cranes to the ceiling,
its paper chain sky dotted with tin stars
and donkey piñatas, none of it close enough
to touch. Today it's tourist-trap fare: rosaries,
ceramic swallows rise and dive—your sisters
just echoes twisting your hand. You're shopping
for a vessel to convey the longing that still
stops you when you least expect a mariachi band,
castanets, how it washes over you, not your life,
but your mother's – a swirl of shawl obscures the present
with glimpses of a misremembered past, R's rolled
in the timpani of her dreams, the thumping
of something beautiful coming that never arrives.
A week later, just back from soccer, your granddaughter
takes the doll from your hand. *Oh, she's pretty*

she says, pushing the mantilla back, peering
into the blank face. She fingers the husk,
studies you from the sliver of the world she commands.
Next time Nana, she says, *you should put a smile right here.*

IV

Why Some Girls Keep Moving

It's just that there are so many
      chairs.   The large one sighs
under my weight   engulfs my fears
      promises to   hold me
        no matter what.   A smaller one
shoves me   forward   onto my toes
     says   *sit up you*   and like
      any hungry child
I keep shifting. Soft chairs   hard
     chairs, chairs that spin. Someplace to
       settle
whatever that means.   Like a matryoshka
     I peel off personas   drape them on furniture
stand there bare   among the hulls.
     It's embarrassing   maybe this one maybe that.

Maybe never.   Frost accumulates
     on the panes.   Sometimes there are
       eyes   in the woods   outside
     sometimes   a girl's voice   whispers
run.

The 605

Most people see freeways as accordions
of time. Breakfast, freeway, work, freeway,
sleep. But some days you and I squeezed
morning and evening together,
left our desks and rushed
toward a laminate table,
fifteen miles for you, ten for me.
By the time I got there
you had ordered.
A cheeseburger each, sleeve of fries to share.
Afterward you kissed me long and salty
through my open window
then slipped back
into the concrete churn.
Whenever I see traffic crawl
through a Los Angeles cloverleaf,
I long to drive the old Subaru west,
while you push the Vega east.
No one noticed me slipping into my chair
at 1:15, a few minutes snatched back
from mornings on the porch,
my lips so hard to pull from yours.
There were days when we were late for work.
Some days we didn't go at all.

Since You Asked

The first time was an act.
I rose from the tumble of clothes
on your living room floor and pulled the drapes
to let in the moon. After that
there were always doors. Bathroom doors,
hotel doors, the door to the house in Irvington,
our heavy bedroom door upstairs,
children sleeping on the other side,
streetlight angled across the walnut bed
as you slid in like a prize, the space between us
merging – first your hands, then mine.
I always loved how you rolled into me,
your smooth shin followed by the pivot
of your hips, though some nights,
I checked the time. Oh, we had fun,
dinners at Bread and Ink, my foot
out of its shoe, or the truck stuck
in the pasture still muddy
from afternoon rain.
Sinatra on the CD, the sound
of a running bath, a certain kind of smile.
These days we don't need to close the door
but do, and these days we sleep.
But since you asked, it's the way
you twined your fingers through my hair
then down my neck and around my back.
How you wrapped your arms to lift me
from the sheet, fingers fanned
over my shoulder blades
like the rest of my wings.

Geyser

A wall of glass separates us
from a canyon of aging high-rises.

Over brunch, my friend's husband
explains how they met: eHarmony.

The two of them brighten the room,
lit only by the glow of half a dozen

bicycles welded into a chandelier.
She beams while I study a column of pigeons

as it erupts into sight. They settle briefly
on wires then cartwheel back to the sidewalk

again and again. The bowl of kale before me
is dotted with Blackened Spam and I lift

a square, slide it into my mouth, thrift enhanced
by craft. When my husband describes the day

we met, lunch hour, quick mart, I nod along.
Married twice as long as our friends, it's hard

not to add, *it hasn't been easy.* The story,
the one we tell, bores me these days,

but look at these birds, how they gush up,
beat the air, fall again to the ground.

Plastic Saints

— Lost Lake, Oregon

Trees line the deserted shore, water
clear enough to track trout, surface

still as an open wound.
Imagine the two of us, how alive

we would be, toes inched forward
to where sand becomes mud, silence

thick as mouthfuls of feathers.
We went once, but we were young

and so dependent on flesh the scenery
withered. If we ever get back there,

we'll rent a boat and float over the water,
like a pair of plastic saints.

Children will watch from campsites
trying to guess whether we were ever alive.

We'll fight to keep our faces straight
while they wonder – the decades falling

like dominoes away.

Orejana

Read that again, I say, and you sigh,
wrap your left hand behind your head,

raise the book in your right. You're
the oldest man I've ever touched now,

though my eye still traces the path
the muscles forge along your arm.

We're reading a history, how my ancestors
lost the ranchos – disrupting their dust

as if they hadn't just settled into the past,
as if their bodies didn't soften as they aged

and learned to forget. This is the chapter
that follows the drought –

rodeos again being arranged, debts
finally paid, though you and I know

every acre will be lost. Our fingers trace
names left behind on graves,

we speak them aloud as if lowing
will lead us back to the herd.

Forty-seven years after my mother's death

I open boxes of her letters and
story floods the corners of the house

until I almost hear her typewriter hum.
Dear Aunt Rosa, she begins, keys clacking.
The wind's been blowing,

the business failing,
a new grandchild due in June.
She watches each character

embed itself in the page.
How quickly she works
while I stand before her desk,

wanting what she cannot give.
I open another carton, withdraw
decades an inch at a time

the warmth of my palms
softening creases as I read.
Love, she types

at the end of each letter.
Then in fine blue ink,
her name.

Praise Poem for Carbon Paper

Praise the delicate sheets of carbon
she slipped between original
and copy. Praise them for serving
again and again, replicating letters
to friends, to lawyers, her stories,
memoranda, memoir. Praise her hands
for twisting the platen, for striking the keys.
Praise the hum of the typewriter,
overture of her mind then the clack,
clack, clack of its music.
Praise the cigarettes ignored
in the green ashtray,
the receiver she clutched
between shoulder and cheek
to write as she talked. Praise her
compound complex sentences,
her purple prose, hyperbole.

At the Beach

Not even a photo but a copy of some dim snapshot
Xeroxed after her funeral. Fifty years later
it's still filed with a list of addresses, some checked,
some not, some labeled pall bearer.

Fourteen years old, two as an orphan, my grandmother
dominates the picture captioned *At the Beach*.
Behind her, arms linked, all the adults that remain
smile for the camera while this girl barely five feet tall

studies the distance like a prophet or a heretic; tiered dress
unbelted, swollen with sea air. I was not yet four
when she died, my memories constructed from stories
like how she tied my hair in rags to make ringlets.

I didn't know she wore them herself, had only seen her
as woman or child, never in between, life washing over her
wave after wave. What caught her gaze that afternoon –
when she thought she had seen the worst and survived?

This year, I've lived four years longer than she did, traced
every part of her life, and nothing would make me snap my fingers
to draw her back to the camera. Nothing could make me
break the spell of whatever caught her eye that afternoon along the shore.

I've finally found the Convent of the Little Flower,

followed the crackling of memory's twigs one diocese
to another until finally I choose an empty pew
make space for the ghosts of my mother and hers.

Three women, one heartbeat in the chapel of a school
where mothers left daughters behind while they mended
broken homes. Now, a congregation of one,

I know the pain its stucco absorbs. My grandmother
grieved her father here, my mother, her parents' divorce.
Countless daughters held fast by catastrophe and the will

of the nuns. My mother talked about knees cushioned
by Kotex, fables invented for sins to confess,
even at the margins of liturgy she laughed. Decades later,

she described watching her mother die, the pursuit
of perfection winding down in soft jolts.
She understood then why she'd been cast away –

her too-brave tongue, round hips, unbecoming drive.
I was probably twelve, a few blocks from home
the day I pulled the hand of the first boy I ever kissed

from my bra. My body didn't yet care, but I could feel
doors opening, good girl, bad girl. Just this once I said no,
testing a lie about mothers and nuns.

Heritage Language

I've lived fifteen years longer than my mother,
longer than any grandmother I can trace.
Their faces remain lineless and mute in photos
though slivers of stories remain.

I scan their faces for gestures,
the way my head tilts, how my hand
wants to rest at my throat.
My mother's Spanish went no further

than commands, *Sientate!, ven aqui!*
She was quoting her mother of course,
who quoted hers, who ran a hotel in Capistrano,
taught the Chinese cook to make tamales.

One of the last Spanish debutantes
in California, she died at 42. The family
appears on a plaque in Heritage Park.
If you look, hers is the first smile you'll see.

Even the lobe of her right ear, visible
beneath upswept hair, beams. No wonder
the cook learned Spanish, her husband converted
to her faith. Now, standing

above her unmarked grave, I fan roses
on the August-dry lawn as if my life atoned
for her unlived years, *lo siento*, I try, *perdóname...,*
lo lamento, hoping one of them is right.

Brother Elegy

— written after hearing Dorianne Laux read "Singer"

My mother didn't set sleeves
on a shapely Singer. Instead,

she used a boxy machine
stamped *Brother*, swore

the whole time. Cut glass
on the dresser, Herb Alpert

on the Hi-Fi, two good dresses
in her closet – her only

extravagance us. *Six dishwashers,*
no lawnmowers, as we flowed

from back seats in identical dresses.
Trial and error she said.

I couldn't tell if it was pride or shame:
so much milk to buy, laundry to wash,

her sink overflowing with dishes.
But you, dear brother I never had,

would not be asked to dry –
already busy being brilliant and tall.

Spitting image of his father,
she would say in the checkout line

while the rest of us stood there
like scenery. She'd order an extra pound

of bacon, lick her thumb, wipe chocolate
from your ruddy cheek.

I don't use flowers in my poems

although I do have two with Peony in the title. They're the only flower I use, except gardenias. And dahlias. A stand of peonies grew alongside the porch of my first home, and my father's last front door was flanked by gardenias. My middle daughter calls herself Dahlia. It's the same thing, really, a woman and the texture of a flower, how the thick petals of gardenias spread themselves flat against their emerald plate. I'm not much of a gardener. I keep the roses going, though they're dormant much of the year. Five bushes wait outside the garage. I drive by every day, notice the first leaves in March, first blooms in May. By October they stand knee deep in their own waste. It's such work to find new ways to describe them when another, even more beautiful, will arrive next spring anyway. But not my sister, bright red petal so full of herself everyone wanted to sink their teeth into her, or the other, clustered close to the ground, a creamy girl with a warm salmon center. They're gone now. It went like this: mother, father, sister, sister, and it just keeps going. I watched a video to try and understand. A rose erupts from its sepals, firm and round, red lips puckered toward morning as slowly it unwinds greedy for sun. Raindrops pearl up like magnifying glasses. The rose in the video yawns wider and wider, until the calyx gives and the first petal falls to the mulch. Then another. The pistils have nothing to do but shiver.

The Way It Is With Us

My mother titled a sheet of paper
Broken Glasses. Her list begins
with Teddy, then me, one glass each.
She never added another name
just the two of us, accomplices
in disappointment. After she died,
I wound up with the one unbreakable
Christmas ornament, a filigree teardrop
filled with spun glass. We called it angel hair,
but Mama said our fingers would bleed
if we touched it. Teddy visited one winter
and said it was hers, that there's a photo
of her hanging it on the tree, but I refused.

This is how it is with us, everything cuts.
In March, we had enchiladas together
for what might be the last time,
each of us a collage of our father's nose,
our mother's hands, her mispronunciation
of salsa. After dinner, the three oldest sisters
line up on the couch, begin the recitation
of bruises, console each other for going first,

while I, youngest by two dead sisters,
study their crows' feet. They don't even notice
when I invoke sisters four and five,
the second half together again.
We're younger than them, faster
than our failing mother. Mary manifests first,
smiles sideways wielding her Marlboro Light.
Jenny rolls her eyes toward the couch,
slides the window open and with a finger to her lips,
tumbles over the sill, into the promise
of a ripe Mojave night.

Headstrong

I learned a horse is a series of circles
from a pamphlet that came in the mail.

Art Instruction, Inc. liked the sketch
my sister sent, praised her talent.

We couldn't afford the lessons, of course,
but now Jenny was *artistic*, code for

not a good student. How I envied her—
already special while I, not yet in trouble

at school, had no future. I tried to keep up
but when I couldn't, I stole the pamphlet.

One big circle forms the horse's jaw,
dotted lines lead to the blunt end

of the muzzle. Jenny's horses had muscle
and skin, manes like waves rolling in.

Their necks arched and dust devils
rose from their hooves. I've had ten extra years

to practice so far, and my horses lie flat
on the page, soulless as marionettes

while hers wait boxed in the closet
already streaked in sweat, haunches crouched,

heads tucked against the bit,
every one of them snorting fire.

Self-Portrait with Big Sister

> ...Like being your mother's baby – you were
> magic, then,
> and not again
>
> "Early Pastoral Aria" – Sharon Olds

From May until August we squatted
in an abandoned house on South and Atlantic.
You cut crystal into half-gram bindles,
skimmed an eighth now and then. I quit my job,
slept on the couch, drove you into the projects
to deliver. Afterward, we sucked the cold
off coconut *paletas* from the *tienda* on South Street.
You wore yourself like a switchblade then,
honed the story of how our mother
put me in your crib

and you on the ground. You called me the parrot –
who sang for parties while you broke windows
just to see if she would look, swallowed oven cleaner,
swiped pennies, cut brown eyes in her direction.
I struggled with the frayed laces of tap shoes
while you hardened into long limbs –
made for looking at,

for taking what she dished out. But all that summer,
we blistered down South Street, crop tops
and low-slung jeans. They'd honk and we'd wave,
spin to watch their cars drive away. Neither of us knew
we searched every face for what we didn't get
from her. But what if I had never been born?
You could have been a child star, then a siren.
I can almost see your brown body lit up
in a turquoise bikini smelling of Coppertone,
Marlboro Lights, and gin. Do you hear the Carpenters
playing on the 8-track, the cocker spaniels
snoring by the kidney-shaped pool?

Punchline

This hurts me more than it hurts you,
how I keep spreading you open
for autopsy, my scalpel sharp
as the one they used
to remove your eyes, the only scrap
still useful.

I want to call the boy who wears
your corneas to ask if he likes shiny things,
if he counts stitches from a distance,
identifies serif, sans serif on billboards,
spots the ich on a guppy before
it infects the tank.

If he classifies boyfriends by mustache –
sluts by the length of their hems.
I wonder if he laughs when he sees a Chihuahua,
if he knows he owes his knack
for stopping a child in its tracks
to you, if his hand hovers over wooden

hangers, if he tests their heft before sliding
on his coat. You used to tell a joke
about a preacher. I thought I would get it by now
but don't. The punchline was: *all he had left
was an organ and a saucer.*
You laughed and laughed.
I'll bet he understands.

Swan Song

When she named me her swan song,
I pictured the bird, though I stood there
with pigtails and fat knees. My mother
didn't know about Cassandra, a captive
who sings a truth no one believes.

No one would hear me.
Even yesterday, all my sisters
on the phone, the curtain kept falling,
tragic as Greek theater. The first time I tried,
the house was on fire. The next time it burned.

Walls kept tumbling down. Now I know
she named me the song and not the swan.
Not the animal but the cry. I thought
I was a prophet, but I'm not, all my words
rootless and unheard.

VI

Object Permanence

My sister's Italian greyhound, already aging
when I visited last, is distressed I've taken her spot
on the sofa. She's thicker than I remember,
my sister's hair gone gray. The years apart
defy summary so we discuss grandchildren,
the garden. Lucy rounds the sofa, stops –
all long legs and angles, directs her milky gaze
toward me, deciphers the air as if code, circles again.
I'm here because our oldest sister's remaining months
rush toward us. The prospect of remission rises,
shatters as Lucy rounds the sofa all balletic dignity,
white legs tipped in daintily clawed knobs.
She swivels a gauzy stare, grumbles, minces past.
My eyes meet my sister's and we find a way to smile,
our faces alike as when she washed and I dried,
or earlier, all six of us flickering on film,
younger girls in matching dresses,
the oldest strumming a guitar.
By the time Lucy rounds the sofa again,
we're comparing prescriptions, frayed fibers
winding tighter around the words our sister has said,
or rather, words said about her, her cells
delinquents wreaking havoc in the blood.
Lucy's chagrin throbs on her refined snout,
its small black tip wrinkling. We've been here before,
know how the world will shudder its hollow tongue.
This time, three of us will remain, half as many oars
propelling a vessel through time. We don't say it

but know, after that there will be two, then one.
Lucy stops mid-orbit, checks the couch,
starts again, hopes next time she goes by,
I'll be gone.

Canyon

From the podium at our sister's funeral,
you lifted your phone to play a voicemail
for everyone to hear. *Are you there?*
she asked, weeks before she died. *Are you*

ignoring me? You were too busy then,
forgot to call back. So her voice broke away
from her life, embedded itself in the skin
of a chip made in China or Taiwan,

fused to fragments of copper wire.
I'm sure you still have it, the way you saved
our grandmother's pin cushion, the bundle of sticks
your son collected. But now you don't answer

when I call. Nurses increase your pain meds,
settle you deeper into your bed. Who will label
the faces in photos? Remind me how lucky
I've been? We sat in folding chairs overlooking

the canyon. Morning mist clung to manzanitas
below. *Are you mad at me?* she asked. *I love you,*
she purred. The music started. A man opened a basket.
A hundred rented doves rushed up then disappeared.

Inventory

Let the stars appear
and the moon disclose her silver horn
        "Let Evening Come" — Jane Kenyon

Where is that old clock with its leaves of brass?
The three-piece sofa, our mother's typewriter
humming on the desk? Where are those things
both silent and voiced that filled the rooms?
How will we anchor ourselves if they can't be found?
Are you sleeping now? Binding memory
back to shadows of things – wobbly table,
bent birdcage, the rocking horse
with its leather ears? Textures you touched
and let go like the briefcase that proved
you a lawyer, the rose bush that proved
you a wife, prom dress, softball bat,
everything borrowed now given back.
Even you, back to your mother,
your father, just the three of you –
the first child, the sharpest tip
of their brand-new star.

Evolution of Things

I never actually mean to go,
but sometimes find myself
at thrift stores, sifting through
remnants flaked from other lives,
all the bits and pieces that wind up
in bins and on shelves. Once,
I bought a perfectly good skillet.
Another time a framed photo
of Santiago Pass. Paperback novels –
barely thumbed, knitting needles, neti pots,
portraits of lap dogs, how grief cascades
through their polka dot bows
and cinnamon eyes, the family unwilling
to grant them space even in the garage.
My sister is dying. She describes the first sign
as a marble burrowing into her breastbone,
a disturbance of the casual composition
of her body, new category of daughter
growing there. They tried to extract it
with subatomic tentacles, sent thousands
of vermillion lashes in to break it loose.
We don't know if it worked,
but the impression left behind is one
of evolution, all of us becoming
something new, yielding space in the drawer
as we move somewhere else. As of now,
everything she owns is precious, but soon
a teenage boy will model the velour jacket

she wore in the 80s, a toddler will clutch
her kewpie doll, a man will push
her progressive lenses up his sunburned nose.

All of Us Eventually

There's always a diagnosis now,
cholesterol, glaucoma, unruly genes
ticking. But we're not talking about me,
we're talking about your father—
how all he will eat these days is
graham crackers and milk.
The morphine, the prowlers
he imagines creeping along the wall.
Or maybe we're talking about all of us
eventually, how everything ends in ashes.
We blended my sister's with her son's,
gray mist in the celebrants' lungs
or you on a chartered boat,
your grandmother's urn –
fishing nets discreetly stowed,
waiting to unfurl, to drag the water
like fingers of memory searching
for a slippery word. Maybe
it will go that way for me,
lid unscrewed, my ashes tipped overboard,
a bloom of jellyfish surfacing.
First, they're sequins rising through dream,
then the edges of ideas pulsate dark
to light, every beautiful thing
I've forgotten, rising.

White Mare

Only if there are angels in your head will you
ever, possibly, see one.
—*Mary Oliver.*

All my horses are dead now.
The Shetland pony, the sorrel,

      the bay. Gone like grandparents
      trailing genes. When I say

that once I rode
very well, I mean

      summer thighs clung
      to the mare's barrel,

our sweat mingling like
blood brothers. I mean

      I first studied my reflection
      in the eye of a horse –

the flea-bitten gray who leaped
tumbleweeds, no saddle, no shoes,

      my hands twisted into mane,
      her hooves striking sand –

one-two, one-two. My heart
falls into rhythm even now.

Acknowledgments

I'm grateful to the following publications and contests for supporting the following poems, sometimes in slightly different forms.

Birdcoat Quarterly —	"Geyser"
Catamaran —	*"Blue Jeans Blues"*
Cider Press Review —	"I don't use flowers in my poems"
Emerson Review —	"Self-Portrait with Big Sister"
Hoxie Gorge —	"Beautiful From a Distance"
Louisville Review —	"Self-Portrait with Spanish Mustang"
Naugatuck Review —	"How Long it Takes to Change Everything" (Narrative Poetry Award Finalist)
Novus Literary Arts Journal —	"Somebody to Love", "Undertow"
Plainsongs —	"All of Us Eventually"
Oberon Review —	"Fledgling"
One Art —	"White Mare"
Quartet —	"Every Morning Leda" (Verse Daily Web Weekly Feature), "Verge" (2025 Quartet Editor's Prize)
Red Rock Review —	"PFC's Tea House" *(Pushcart Nomination, 2022)*
Rust + Moth —	"Orejana"
San Pedro River Review —	"Origin Story"
Sheila-Na-Gig —	"Brother Elegy", "All Mothers are Mythologies"
The Shore —	"Viceroy"

<table>
<tr><td>Sugar House Review</td><td>—</td><td>"Why Some Girls Keep Moving"</td></tr>
<tr><td>Watershed Review</td><td>—</td><td>"Madre Dura"</td></tr>
<tr><td>West Trade Review</td><td>—</td><td>"La Linea", "Punchline"</td></tr>
<tr><td>Whale Road Review</td><td>—</td><td>"Object Permanence"</td></tr>
</table>

About the Author

Melody Wilson is a Pushcart nominated poet whose work appears in *Willow Springs, Calyx, One, The Emerson Review*, *Nimrod, Rust and Moth*, and many other publications. Her awards include an Academy of American Poets Prize, the Patricia Dobler Award, and others. She is founder of the poetry collective Zalon and teaches poetry for Portland Community College both in traditional classrooms and the correctional setting. A graduate of Pacific University's MFA program, she lives in Portland, Oregon with her husband Phillip and their dog Z. Find more of her work at melodywilson.com.

www.ingramcontent.com/pod-product-compliance
Lightning Source LLC
Chambersburg PA
CBHW032122050726

47590CB00008B/2925